VIRGO

23 August – 22 September

Abbeydale Press

Virgo is the sixth Sun Sign . . .

1. Aries, The Ram: 21 March–19 April
2. Taurus, The Bull: 20 April–20 May
3. Gemini, The Twins: 21 May–20 June
4. Cancer, The Crab: 21 June–22 July
5. Leo, The Lion: 23 July–22 August
6. Virgo, The Virgin: 23 August–22 September
7. Libra, The Scales: 23 September–22 October
8. Scorpio, The Scorpion: 23 October–21 November
9. Sagittarius, The Archer: 22 November–21 December
10. Capricorn, The Goat: 22 December–19 January
11. Aquarius, The Water Carrier: 20 January–18 February
12. Pisces, The Fishes: 19 February–20 March

© 1999 Bookmart Limited

All rights reserved. No part of this publication may be reproduced, stored in a retrieval system or transmitted by any means, electronic, mechanical, photocopying or otherwise, without the prior permission of the publisher.
Published by Abbeydale Press
An imprint of Bookmart Limited. Registered Number 2372865.
Trading as Bookmart Limited, Desford Road,
Enderby, Leicester LE9 5AD, UK.

ISBN 1-86147-0371

Produced for Bookmart by Scribble Ink,
4 The Old Maltings, Hopton, Suffolk IP22 2QZ, UK.
Telephone: 01953 681564. Fax: 01953 681574.
Printed in Singapore.

The word ASTROLOGY comes from two Greek words – *astron* (star) and *logos* (knowledge). Astrology is based on a belief that there is a definable link between patterns in the heavens and patterns here on Earth. Astrologers use the positions of stars and planets at the time of an individual's birth to predict certain influences that will shape the character and subsequent life of that person. By compiling a detailed birthchart (or horoscope), they then seek to determine positive and negative forces likely to apply to that individual.

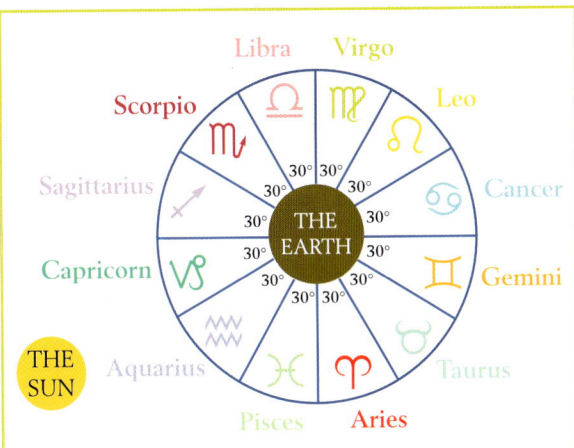

The starting point for astrology is the Zodiac Wheel. The wheel is an imaginary band around Earth, divided into 12 segments of 30°. Each segment is named after a nearby star constellation, and everyone born when the Sun is passing through that segment has the appropriate "Sun Sign".

INTRODUCTION:

DO HOROSCOPES actually work? Many people regard astrology as no more than a bit of harmless fun – but deep inside even the most cynical lurks a primitive suspicion that there may be more to this ancient art than they care to admit.

The birth of astrology is lost in the mists of time. The earliest known horoscopes emerged in Babylonia around 500 BC, and serious study of the stars began with the Greek philosopher Ptolemy's book *Almagest* in the 2nd Century.

Over the years, this work was built upon by many great thinkers, including Abu Ma'shar (Persia), Guido Bonatti and Marsilio Ficino (Italy) and Nicolaus Copernicus (Poland). By the 16th Century the principles of astrology were firmly established and Queen Elizabeth I's court astrologer, John Dee, was a respected figure.

As technology improved, studying the stars split into two disciplines: astronomy and astrology –

YOUR FATE IN THE STARS?

the latter dismissed by scientists on the grounds that its conclusions could not be proved.

Scientific or not, astrology continued to fascinate and new knowledge of the heavens was put to good use in developing the detailed theories that underpin modern astrology.

Because everyone born under Virgo has a unique birthchart, each will have a different astrological "destiny" in store. For example, a strong physical connection with matters relating to the intestines can manifest itself as a strength or a weakness (or neither!), depending on the person concerned. And even some of the most general traits associated with Virgo may be absent if other, more powerful influences are present in an individual's horoscope.

This pocket guide is designed to summarise the main Virgoan characteristics and influences. Check them out and decide for yourself if the stars have got it right!

ZODIAC BRIEFING:

PLANETS

Every Sun Sign is associated with, and ruled by, one or more of the 10 astrological planets, each of which exerts specific influence on the sign(s) it rules – and any birthcharts in which it appears. Virgo is ruled by Mercury.

⊙	SUN	*The Sun provides the energy at the heart of our solar system. It represents the vital life force within everyone, symbolising authority, pride, strength and courage.*
☽	MOON	*The Moon complements the bold qualities of the Sun, standing for the rhythms of emotional life, nurturing qualities and a person's relationship with their body.*
☿	MERCURY	*Swift-orbiting Mercury represents quick and enquiring thinking, communication and commerce. Also linked with less desirable traits like cunning and crime.*
♀	VENUS	*Venus shares the female circle-and-cross glyph, and is the planet associated with grace, love and beauty. It can also represent vanity and a desire for luxuries.*
♂	MARS	*Blood-red Mars shares the male circle-and-arrow glyph, and represents direct energy and ambition. It suggests positive qualities like heroism, but also selfishness.*
♃	JUPITER	*The largest planet, Jupiter, stands for self-confidence, adventure, exploration and expansion. Jupiter can also influence good athletic ability and risk-taking.*
♄	SATURN	*Once thought to be the outermost planet, Saturn is the planet of order, self-discipline, security and duty. Linked with the skeleton, which gives the body form.*
♅	URANUS	*Uranus – discovered only in 1781 – represents social change, dramatic upheavals and rapid technological advance. A strong influence for all sorts of innovation.*
♆	NEPTUNE	*The secret world of imagination, dreams, spirituality and fantasy is associated with Neptune. Traditionally linked with the sea and its mysterious depths.*
♇	PLUTO	*Late-on-the-scene Pluto represents life's darker forces and is connected to war, pestilence and death. More positively, it influences regeneration after destruction.*

THE KEY INFLUENCES

ELEMENTS

The astrological world consists of four basic elements – Fire, Earth, Air and Water. Each exerts its own distinctive influence on a horoscope, and rules three Sun Signs, imparting its elemental character to those signs. Virgo is an Earth Sign.

FIRE
Fire crackles and burns like a relentless spirit, providing a symbol for human enthusiasm, energy and drive to achieve.

EARTH
The Earth is the solid core of our being and stands for all that is reliable, unchanging, predictable and material in life.

AIR
Think of a bird soaring free as a metaphor for Air, which thus represents the freedom of ideas, thought, and communication.

WATER
Water finds its own level, often flowing in mysterious ways as an ideal symbol for inner feelings, emotions and the human soul.

QUALITIES

The 12 Sun Signs are divided among three essential qualities – Cardinal, Fixed and Mutable. The Cardinal Quality supports activity and initiative. The Fixed Quality indicates reliability and stability. The Mutable Quality stands for adaptability and change. Virgo is a Mutable Sign.

GENDER

Each Sun Sign is either "masculine" or "feminine". This is not a direct link with sexuality, but rather an indication of a general approach to life. The masculine (positive) signs are associated with an outgoing, assertive disposition and the feminine (negative) signs are associated with an intuitive, receptive character. Virgo is a feminine sign.

ZODIAC BRIEFING:

SUN SIGN	QUALITY	GLYPH
1. ARIES	Cardinal	♈
2. TAURUS	Fixed	♉
3. GEMINI	Mutable	♊
4. CANCER	Cardinal	♋
5. LEO	Fixed	♌
6. VIRGO	Mutable	♍
7. LIBRA	Cardinal	♎
8. SCORPIO	Fixed	♏
9. SAGITTARIUS	Mutable	♐
10. CAPRICORN	Cardinal	♑
11. AQUARIUS	Fixed	♒
12. PISCES	Mutable	♓

SUMMARY OF INFLUENCES

ELEMENT	GENDER	RULING PLANET
Fire	Masculine	Mars
Earth	Feminine	Venus
Air	Masculine	Mercury
Water	Feminine	The Moon
Fire	Masculine	The Sun
Earth	Feminine	Mercury
Air	Masculine	Venus
Water	Feminine	Mars/Pluto
Fire	Masculine	Jupiter
Earth	Feminine	Saturn
Air	Masculine	Uranus/Saturn
Water	Feminine	Neptune/Jupiter

VIRGO:

THE MAIDEN is the symbol of Virgo and she represents the self-contained and self-sufficient character of typical Virgoans, who have natural modesty and independence. Virgo is an analytical sign and its members are careful people who constantly strive for perfection.

Because perfection is hard to achieve, Virgoans are often disappointed and tend to be critical – of themselves and others. Mostly themselves. They worry about their shortcomings, real or imagined, and are rarely satisfied by standards achieved. So they may work compulsively, often to conceal a fundamental concern that they're unworthy and flawed.

It sounds dour, but isn't all bad. Virgoans have quick – sometimes brilliant – minds. They take great satisfaction in serving others and calmly handle a large volume of necessary, worthwhile work that might otherwise remain undone.

Personally, Virgoans are good communicators

THE VIRGIN

whose thoughts are usually shrewd and give sound advice. Though hard working, typically appearing fairly passive and modest, they are honest, have real strength of character, take responsibility readily and are unstinting in their service to others.

POSITIVE VIRGOAN QUALITIES
- *Gentle and kind to those weaker than themselves*
- *Organised, efficient and good under pressure*
- *Charming, amusing and very sympathetic*
- *Emotional warmth and ill-disguised sensuality*

NEGATIVE VIRGOAN QUALITIES
- *Tendency to worry and become very irritable*
- *Cruelly critical of any second-rate performance*
- *Can be untidy and disorganised in personal life*
- *Emotional detachment, bad at expressing feelings*

oooooo LUCKY LINKS oooooo

Colours – Lime green, dark brown, cream
Gemstones – Agate, opal

VIRGO MAN,

VIRGO MAN

If typical, with no forces in his birthchart that outweigh the natural influence of his Sun Sign, the Virgoan male will show some or all of these key characteristics . . .

- *Stands physically upright and often quite tall*
- *Has a genuine love of work and responsibility*
- *Apparently unemotional, rarely sentimental*
- *Possesses excellent practical skills and abilities*
- *Can be very subtle in pursuing his objectives*
- *Has a dry sense of humour, can be sarcastic*

VIRGO WOMAN

The typically Virgoan woman, if ruled by her Sun Sign rather than contradictory influences in her birthchart, will show some or all of these key characteristics . . .

- *Always looks well groomed and neatly dressed*
- *Tireless worker and considers herself efficient*
- *Shy and reserved, but enjoys helping others*
- *Has open, honest and uncomplicated personality*
- *Finds it hard to express emotions and feelings*
- *Not easily deflected from chosen course of action*

WOMAN & CHILD

VIRGO CHILD

A characteristic young Virgoan is quick to learn, often talking and reading early. Sensitive if teased and shy with strangers. Self-effacing and may be bullied in consequence, often countering with self-parodying humour. Honest, reliable and unlikely to question authority.

Attraction of opposites?

Virgoans are rarely drawn to members of the opposite and complementary sign – though Pisceans offer the imagination that can add a valuable dimension to the Virgoan work ethic.

VIRGO:

FRIENDSHIP is an orderly business for the typical Virgoan. Friends will not often be emotional types, because Virgoans prefer calmer sorts with intelligent awareness of many and varied subjects, and willingness to discuss them.

When it comes to those who share their wide-ranging interests and analytical approach to life, Virgoans can make loyal, helpful and committed friends. Though the number of close friends is likely to be few, the Virgoan may well be on good but not intimate terms with a large circle of acquaintances, enjoying spirited exchanges of casual banter.

Heaven help the friend who tries to make a Virgoan admit that he or she might be wrong – it's simply not in the Virgoan character to make such a damning confession. Yet they themselves can become hyper-critical, occasionally upsetting friends with caustic or barbed comments.

Family life is very important to Virgoans. They

FRIENDS & FAMILY

may work like Trojans, but home is the place where they can let their hair down and truly relax. And whilst a Virgoan will typically love the practical side of running and maintaining an orderly household, it is interacting with the people in that home that really matters.

Never one to express emotions effusively, the Virgoan nonetheless has a great need to find the ability to feel and give love – and it's the family that becomes the main beneficiary of success.

VIRGO PARENTS

The parent whose birthchart has a typically Virgo pattern, without contradictory influences, will show some or all of these key characteristics when raising children . . .

- *Will do anything to help and support children*
- *Prefers reasoned argument to issuing orders*
- *Likes helping with projects or homework*
- *Believes in stimulating children's curiosity*
- *Can be over-concerned about children's health*
- *Finds it hard to express affection physically*

VIRGO:

CATS AND BIRDS don't get on well, though every so often newspapers will publish a picture of a canary sitting happily on moggy's head – a good story precisely because it is a perfect example of the unexpected.

So it is with people born under the different signs of the zodiac. It's possible to calculate how well (or badly!) Virgos should relate to members of every other Sun Sign, and the results are shown opposite.

Generally, signs that share the same element – Fire, Air, Earth or Water – relate harmoniously, as will those sharing one of the three qualities – Cardinal, Fixed or Mutable. When it comes to the ruling planets, however, relationships with members of the opposing sign are usually quite difficult – so Virgos should beware of Pisceans bearing gifts!

But remember, there will always be those striking attractions of opposites that prove the rule.

RELATIONSHIPS

Virgo Relationship Chart

The chart shows how well a typical Virgo relates to those born under all 12 Sun Signs. Check to see if your own personal relationships show a marked Virgoan compatibility pattern . . .

Rating =	Easy	Hard	Stressful
ARIES			✘
TAURUS	✔		
GEMINI		?	
CANCER	✔		
LEO	✔		
VIRGO	✔		
LIBRA	✔		
SCORPIO	✔		
SAGITTARIUS		?	
CAPRICORN	✔		
AQUARIUS			✘
PISCES		?	

VIRGO:

THE VIRGIN is chaste, but that doesn't apply to those born under her Sun Sign. Instead, she symbolises fertility. Yet it's true that Virgoans male and female can often seem shy when it comes to love – even timid. Don't be fooled. They are adept at using this as a subtle weapon of seduction, and beneath the modesty lies veiled sensuality.

But Virgoan love is not about torrid sexuality. Instead, Virgoans extend their caring side to include family, friends and even anyone who is in trouble. Virgoans want to feel they are needed, and capable of opening their hearts by responding to others. It's a powerful combination of duty, devotion and emotion.

No Virgoan will commit to a relationship they expect to fail. They're not generally promiscuous, even in young adulthood, and can wait years for the right person to come along, albeit with a few tentative trial runs along the way. Once they're settled, the commitment is absolute and

LOVE & SEX

they will do everything that's humanly possible to nurture and sustain the relationship . . . except wearing their hearts on their sleeves.

Sexually, Virgoans are open-minded and regard making love as a wonderful opportunity to express the love they find so hard to define in words . . . and cast aside the inhibitions that impose stern discipline on the rest of their lives.

VIRGO LOVERS

Where strong Virgo influence dominates the birthchart, a Virgoan in love will show all or some of these characteristics . . .

- *Undemonstrative, but devoted to his/her partner*
- *Very private and secretive about personal life*
- *Faithful and rarely (if ever) tempted to stray*
- *Expects partner to understand unspoken feelings*
- *Can be turned off if expected to be romantic*
- *Hates hypocrisy or lies within a relationship*
- *Will sustain love with unswerving commitment*
- *Can be modest or even prudish about sex*
- *Goes to any lengths to avoid breaking up*

VIRGO:

Virgo is a sign associated with the ability to sift through everything in detail and there's a strong physical link with the intestines, the body's own processing mechanism.

Although Virgos are typically healthy, they may not always see it that way themselves, often showing signs of hypochondria, especially when worried or stressed. The positive side of this is a marked tendency to look after themselves well, with a sensible diet and keep fit regime.

The Virgo is a restless type, needing to keep busy to avoid the possibility of sinking into introverted depression, though when inactivity becomes mentally threatening they are quick to counter the effects by changing course.

Virgos usually make very good patients when sick – requiring only minimal fuss, attention and encouragement to help a speedy recovery.

HEALTH & FITNESS

Typical illnesses are digestive in character – diarrhoea, ulcers, appendicitis, indigestion – or associated with the lymph system, whilst spleen problems are not uncommon. Virgo the worrier may become a compulsive fingernail chewer,

Strengths & Weaknesses

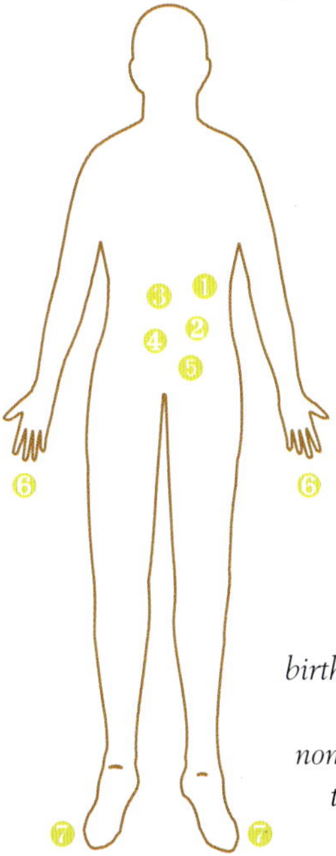

KEY

1. Spleen
2. Duodenum
3. Abdominal Organs
4. Intestines
5. Colon
6. Fingernails
7. Toenails

Depending on their own birthcharts, individuals may show either strength or weakness in none, some or all of these parts of the body that are traditionally associated with Virgo.

VIRGO:

VIRGOANS at work are like fish in water. It's their natural habitat, allowing them to express their meticulous nature fully and pursue that elusive dream of perfection. They enjoy all sorts of complex administration, but can gain equal satisfaction by discharging routine work efficiently and with a minimum of fuss.

Ideal jobs are in fields like charity work, general administration, secretarial, banking, bookkeeping, accountancy, small business, medicine, pharmacy . . . literally anywhere (which is almost everywhere) that needs disciplined Virgoan skills to keep the wheels turning smoothly.

As a boss, the Virgoan man or woman isn't a natural front person, not being at their best in dealing with clients or public. But they make good bosses of smaller enterprises where an all-seeing eye for detail, fiscal acumen and clear analytical thinking can pay off. They are honest and very reasonable employers who expect politeness and a fair day's work from their

WORK & PLAY

employees, in return for which they will pay a fair day's wage.

Virgoan workers are at their best in responsible supporting positions, bringing stability and order to the most tangled tasks. Given a choice, they prefer to be of service to others. But their analytical thinking, efficient performance and reliability can be an asset in almost any role.

VIRGO LEISURE

Where primary Virgo influence predominates in a birthchart, the Virgoan at play will show all or some of these characteristics . . .

- *Slight guilt at taking time out for mere pleasure*
- *Lack of interest in playing competitive sport*
- *Strong interest in practical home improvement*
- *Likes creative hobbies producing tangible result*
- *Drawn to anything concerning arts and literature*
- *Enjoys pastimes that can stimulate the mind*
- *Loves home computing and surfing the Net*
- *May pursue adult education, self-improvement*
- *Keen on activities involving family or friends*

A–Z KEYWORDS

ASCENDANT (or RISING SIGN) – the point on the eastern horizon of a zodiac birthchart.
ASPECT – the angle in degrees between planets in a birthchart.
ASTROLOGY – the study of relationships (or "coincidences" in modern parlance) between actual events and planetary positions at the time.
BIRTHCHART (or HOROSCOPE) – chart that calculates the positions of Sun, Moon and planets at the time and place of an individual's birth, representing a combination unique to that person.
CELESTIAL SPHERE – that view of the heavens seen from Earth, as though Earth were the centre of the Universe.
CONJUNCTION – term used when two or more planets are positioned close together in a birthchart.
CUSP – point at which two houses of a birthchart adjoin, often allowing influences associated with another Sun Sign to impact on an individual's horoscope.
DESCENDANT (or FALLING SIGN) – the point on the western horizon of a zodiac birthchart.
ELEMENT – the four elements of Fire, Air, Earth and Water are linked with general characteristics that apply to related zodiac signs.
FORECAST – Attempt to predict the future based on previous planetary patterns and their known future positions.
GENDER – the 12 Sun Signs are equally divided between the "masculine" and "feminine" genders, symbolising aspects generally associated with the male and female character respectively.
GLYPH – symbol representing Sun Sign, planet etc.
PLANET – eight major bodies excluding Earth that move around the Sun. The Sun and Moon are included to make 10 "astrological" planets. Each planet "governs" one or more Sun Signs, imparting its own characteristics.
QUALITY – the 12 Sun Signs are equally divided between three essential qualities, Cardinal, Fixed and Mutable, each with distinct impact on the relevant signs.
SUN SIGN – that sign of the zodiac occupied by the Sun on an individual's date of birth (often incorrectly termed "star sign").
ZODIAC – imaginary spectrum that divides the solar system into 12 segments, each named after a constellation of stars close by.
ZODIAC SIGNS – the 12 segments of the zodiac, numbered in an anticlockwise direction, based on their positions at the spring equinox.